KICKSTART

Interactive
Leader's Manual

2nd Edition © 2009 Ruth Lewis
First published 2008
Published by Envision Publishing
27 Glebe Villas, Hove BN3 5SL

Please respect the authors rights. Please do not copy,
duplicate or change without the author's permission

Unless otherwise indicated, all Scripture quotations are taken from the Holy Bible, NEW LIVING TRANSLATION, copyright © 1996, 2004. Used by permission of Tyndale House Publishers, INC., Wheaton, Illinois 60189. All rights reserved.

Scripture quotations marked "NKJV™" are taken from the New King James Version®. Copyright © 1982 by Thomas Nelson, Inc. Used by permission. All rights reserved.

Scripture quotations marked (AMP) are taken from the Amplified Bible, Copyright © 1954, 1958, 1962, 1964, 1965, 1987 by The Lockman Foundation. Used by permission.

ISBN: 978-0-9564056-5-4

CONTENTS

Leader's Guidelines	iii
Bible Exploration	1
Spiritual Languages	3
Significant Prayer	5
Practical Prophecy	7
Words Of Knowledge	9
Worship	11
Powerful Testimony	13
Spiritual Purpose	15
Positive Influence	17
Recap/Review/Refocus	19
Suggested Reading	20
About the Author/About CityCoast Church	21

LEADER'S GUIDELINES

As with other KickStart courses, the Interactive course works best in a group setting with space to break up into smaller groups for activities.

It is beneficial to encourage the group to write notes in their books and to study between sessions. Each session has a few introductory notes, Bible verses and keys. It is up to the leader to decide how much these are used and elaboration and development of the sections can vary depending on the nature and make-up of the group.

The main learning sections of KickStart Interactive are, however, the activities and practical sessions. Within education it is well recognised that we often learn more effectively through activity and discussion than we do through listening alone, and this is the main purpose of this course. It is good to keep this at the forefront of planning for each session. Remember, it is very easy to slip into telling rather than allowing the group to discover truth and practical out working of their relationship with God.

Within this leader's manual ideas have been given for activities and the practical parts, but feel free to add to these and be as creative as appropriate in order to fulfil the outcomes that the session presents.

It is good to ask the group questions rather than make statements. Allowing discussion within the group will help everyone even if they don't all participate to the same extent. However, it is important to summarise discussions in order to bring the key points and Biblical truth at the end. If strong disagreements surface, help people to understand that we may not agree on everything - only on central doctrinal points must we be definite.

In order to help the change process and positive development of our lives, a section for action plans has also been included. For each session encourage the group to consider at least one thing to do or change in their life following this session and write it down, so that they are taking steps towards becoming more fully who God intended them to be. Take some time at the next session to report back on experiences.

Finally, remember to enjoy the sessions with the group. It is intended to be a course that also builds relationships and is fun as more of our Spirit life is discovered together.

1. Bible EXPLORATION

"Let the WORD spoken by Christ the Messiah have its home in your hearts and minds and dwell in you in all its richness as you teach and train one another in all insight, intelligence and wisdom in spiritual things"

Colossians 3:16 (AMP)

INTRODUCTION

God so desires to communicate with us so we can know Him and His will for our lives, the church and the world.

The Bible was written over centuries, by those He communicated with, for everyone down though history to explore. It is a gift from God to us.

A general reading of the Bible (or Word of God) shows us what happened in history relating to the beginning of time, the next few hundred years, the Jewish people, the life, death and resurrection of Jesus, and the beginning of the church. It also contains what prophets were saying during parts of history, proverbs about life (King Solomon), psalms which are like poetry or songs (mainly by King David) and a prophetic book (Revelation) about the things to come in the future.

The Bible, however, is more than just a book. The Holy Spirit works with every believer to show them truth through the words (generally and specifically) and bring about what they (the words) say/mean, in their lives and circumstances. We are changed by the Word of God and the Holy Spirit.

As the Holy Spirit wants to speak to us through the Bible and desires that it impacts us and what we do, we must give Him the opportunity to do so by studying/looking at it in a deeper way.

THE BIBLE SAYS

1 Peter 1:25   Hebrews 4:12   Jeremiah 23:29   Psalm 119:18

KEYS FOR STUDYING THE BIBLE

When studying a verse or part of the Bible consider :

- Who was it written by?
- Why was it written?
- Who was it written for?
- What is God saying?
- Does this reveal anything about God's character?
- Is there a promise of God for me?
- Is there a commandment of God for me to follow?

Ask the Holy Spirit to show you things, to help you understand and to direct you as you read. Don't rush. It is quality not quantity that is usually the best way to look at the Bible.

ACTIVITY 1: Psalm 37:1-5

LEADER'S NOTE:

Provide some Bibles - different translations.

Read the section in a few translations and encourage the group to look for the main themes/overview. Divide the group into pairs or small groups and divide the verses up between the groups. Ask them to discuss the verses asking the questions:

What is God saying?

How does this apply to our lives?
[10 minutes]

Ask each group to report back.

Summarise what the passage is saying, how it applies to us, how it can be involved in our prayer etc. Encourage the group to study the Bible this way on their own regularly, praying that the Holy Spirit will speak through the Word and writing down the truth that is revealed.

ACTIVITY 2: Theme Study

LEADER'S NOTE:

Provide resources such as Bibles, concordances, Bible commentary and Christian reference books. Explain how to use them and challenge each pair or small group to find some verses on a subject, e.g. love.

ACTIVITY 3: Character Study

LEADER'S NOTE:

Discuss which characters from the Bible could be studied and how.
Brainstorm this as a whole group and encourage them to do this at some time in the future.

ACTION PLAN

LEADER'S NOTE:

Spend some time summarising what has been done and encourage the group to make one action plan each for the week regarding Bible study and to write it down.

2. Spiritual LANGUAGES

"Now I wish that you might ALL speak in unknown tongues"

1 Corinthians 14:5a (AMP)

INTRODUCTION

Tongues or speaking in other languages is from God - a gift from the Father via the Holy Spirit. It is available when we become baptised in the Holy Spirit. It is a language that we haven't learnt and our minds won't neccessarily understand. We do, however, have control over when we use it.

Tongues begin much like any language and grow as we use them. Many sounds, words and phrases will be heard and the type of tongue or the language may change when the gift is used for different purposes, e.g. worship, praying for others, warfare against the devil's plans.

Tongues may be spiritual (or heavenly) languages or recognised natural languages. They can be used all the time, but at times God will ask us to speak in a tongue for a message to others. This will either be interpreted or recognised as another language by the recipient/s and therefore understood.

Tongues are available for all who believe!

THE BIBLE SAYS

Acts 2   Acts 10   1 Corinthians 12:10   Ephesians 6:18   1 Corinthians 14:14,15

KEYS FOR PRAYING IN TONGUES

- Practise using tongues by repeating sounds that come at first then allow new ones to be added as you move your mouth to speak out what is growing in your spirit.
- Focus on God or what you are praying about.
- Don't let your mind wander.
- Worship God with tongues - this is your spirit giving worship to God in expressions beyond what your mind could think.
- As you pray, use tongues either for a time on their own or dispersed among your natural language.
- Ask the Holy Spirit to expand/vary your tongues and to use them to bring about the will of God.
- Use tongues when you do not know what to pray and trust God for the best answers and outcomes.
- Pray until you feel to stop.

ACTIVITY: The Purpose Of Tongues

LEADER'S NOTE:

Either ask the group to split into pairs or they can do this individually. Ask them to write down why they think God gives us the ability to speak in tongues. What are tongues for?

Expected responses - tongues are used for:

- Worship
- Prayer (alongside natural language)
- When we don't know what to pray
- Making us stronger spiritually
- Warfare
- Giving a message from God

PRACTICAL

Pray together using tongues. Recap to the group, as necessary, our use of tongues as we pray.
Lead them in prayer.
Suggested plan:

- All pray in tongues together (focus on God and worship)
- Thank and praise God (use native language and tongues)
- Ask the Holy Spirit to come - to fill us, guide us, increase His work in us, increase our tongues...
- Pray more in tongues together
- Pray about a specific subject relevant to your group/church/situation. Use own language and tongues giving explanation as appropriate and focusing on using tongues in different ways.
- Pray for each person for more of the Spirit and for more release in tongues.

N. B. This session is carried out as above assuming the group have studied KickStart 1 and 2 regarding the Holy Spirit and His gifts/manifestation in Christians, are familiar with experiencing tongues in church settings, and have all been baptised in the Holy Spirit. More explanation of prayer with some individuals may be required if this is not the case. This session is to encourage the participants to go further in the area of tongues and prayer.

ACTION PLAN

LEADER'S NOTE:

Encourage the group to consider how they can build the use of the gift of tongues in their lves and to write down at least one action they will take.

3. Significant PRAYER

"Pray in the Spirit at all times and on every occasion. Stay ALERT and be persistent in your prayers for all believers everywhere"
Ephesians 6:18

INTRODUCTION

Prayer is the basis of our relationship with God individually and as Christians together (the church).

Prayer is communication – speaking, listening, non-verbal and verbal expression. Worship, intimate language, sharing feelings, communicating about circumstances, asking, confessing wrong, speaking Scripture and silence are all part of our personal relationship expressed through prayer.

Prayer is also about partnering with God against or for something using Scriptures, words in line with Scripture and declarations. We help to accomplish God's will on earth and the Holy Spirit leads us in this as we pray, using our natural language and tongues (spiritual language).

Prayer is very significant and vital to the life of a believer and significant to what happens in the world.

THE BIBLE SAYS

Proverbs 15:8b   James 5:13-16   Isaiah 56:7 1 Timothy 2:8
Philippians 4:6   1 Thessalonians 5:17

ACTIVITY: Mind map

LEADER'S NOTE:

Give the group a few minutes to consider prayer. Using the mind map each person can put down anything they connect with prayer, e.g.

KEYS FOR PRAYER

- Remember we can talk to God at anytime and any place.
- Set aside some focused time on a regular basis to talk to and listen to God, as well as to pray about situations and pray in tongues.
- Having a place without distractions helps.
- Consider what we have done today and ask the Holy Spirit to develop prayer in your life.
- Go and be part of a prayer meeting and learn from others as well as participating with them.
- Have your Bible with you when you pray and use Scriptures in prayer - maybe find some appropriate verses that you want to pray.
- Use a psalm to help you worship God in prayer, e.g. Psalm 103.
- Don't stop praying until you feel "released" to do so (in other words you get the sense you have finished).

ACTION PLAN

LEADER'S NOTE:

Discuss with the group how it is important for prayer to become a regular and significant part of our lives. Encourage the group to discuss in pairs what prayer plan they could put into their lives. Each individual can write down their ideas.

Possible ideas:

- Pray each day for a set amount of time
- Pray in different ways at different times
- Use a prayer journal
- Pray with another person regularly

Encourage the group to be specific, e.g. not 'pray more' but 'pray for 10 minutes 4 times a week and once a week with my friend for half a hour.

PRACTICAL

Lead a time of prayer. Incorporate aspects of prayer including: worship, thanksgiving, intercession, declaration and warfare. Use tongues and Scripture where appropriate.

Make sure the group learns how to engage, follow and contribute as well as learning about the different aspects of prayer and practising them.

N. B. This will help individuals learn about prayer that will help them individually, but it will also encourage and develop their ability to pray with a group. Some explanation about following and contribution may need to be brought in a way that is appropriate to your church's form of group prayer.

4. Practical PROPHECY

*"So, my brethren, earnestly desire and **set your hearts** on **prophesying** (on being inspired to preach and teach and to interpret God's will and purpose)."*

1 Corinthians 14:39a (AMP)

IINTRODUCTION

Throughout history God has been speaking. From "let there be light" right up to today God has used words containing creative power to bring about what He speaks. He speaks through the Bible, further through prophecy and directly into our hearts as the Holy Spirit is involved in our lives.

When we are baptised or filled (a continuous thing) with the Holy Spirit we have the ability to prophesy just as we are enabled to speak in tongues. Prophecy is to be as normal and available to us as any other thing the Holy Spirit wants to do in us.

Prophecy is mainly used to encourage and reinforce what God is doing specifically in or for someone, and is always in line with what the Bible says.

Just as with anything of God, this gift can grow and develop as we use it and God can use us to speak more specifically and accurately about situations, circumstances and direction. As we learn and grow in prophecy we do so under covering and the guidance of leaders that God gives us, for protection of ourselves and others.

The Holy Spirit anoints (gives special ability to) some specifically to use prophecy and some he gives the "office" of a prophet, just as some are specifically gifted to be evangelists and some to be teachers.

THE BIBLE SAYS

1 Corinthians 12:4-10,28   1 Corinthians 13:21   Corinthians 14:1-5,12   Isaiah 55:11

ACTIVITY: What have you heard about/seen of prophecy?

LEADER'S NOTE:

In small groups ask the group to discuss their own experiences of what they have heard or seen about prophecy. They may mention instances from within a church setting or from ungodly sources, e.g. fortune telling. Encourage the groups to write down as many examples as possible and then discuss their feelings and responses. Allow time for each group to report on their discussions.

N. B. Some may find prophecy a bit scary or think that it is only for certain people who they may consider to be "more spiritual". Encourage the group to remember that prophecy is for all, quoting Paul who desired that "all should prophesy".

[This activity may work well as the first part of the session before anything else is said about prophecy.]

KEYS FOR PROPHECY

- God gave us an imagination. Allow the Holy Spirit to use it.
- Ask Him to show you things about yourself or situations.
- As you picture something expect Him to show you the meaning behind the picture and how it applies to your life or something/someone else.
- You may not "see" a picture but you may become aware of a word or phrase that you believe comes from God, i.e. He is communicating.
- Prophecy is mainly for encouragement and positively helps someone else.

PRACTICAL - How does God see me at the moment?

Before beginning this activity, explain how God often communicates with us prophetically by using our imagination to show us "pictures".

Go through the following with the group:

Imagine a dog
- The dog is red
- The dog is barking
- Have a look at what it is barking at

Some in the group will respond with what they "see". Ask if anyone couldn't "see" the dog. If all are able to do this, proceed. If not, go through similar exercises to help the group use their imaginations.

All pray in tongues together (focus on God and worship)

Write down a picture or word God shows you:
What does this mean?

In a few minutes silence give the group time to write down what God shows them about themselves and what it might mean. Invite the group to discuss their results.

Write down a picture or word God shows you about another person:
What does this mean?

Repeat this considering someone else in the room. As leader of the group it is important to help support and guide this - what is seen and the interpretation - making sure it is Biblical, encouraging and positive. Draw on the Holy Spirit who is wanting to communicate with us.

ACTION PLAN

LEADER'S NOTE:
Encourage the group to write down at least one way to grow in the prophetic this week.

5. Words of KNOWLEDGE

"...to one is given... the word of knowledge through the same Spirit."
1 Corinthians 12:8 (NKJV)

INTRODUCTION

As we have said already, God wants to communicate. He desires relationship with us. He also wants to help and support us in our lives, and for us to do the same for others as He leads and works through us.

God communicates with us through our prayer relationship, the Bible, prophecy, teaching from others etc. Much of what He "says" is for us but also He will give us knowledge about a situation, circumstance or person that we are to pass on/act upon.

When we receive a specific revelation from Him for someone else, that we did not know from any other source, it is called a "word of knowledge".

God can use any of us to give a word of knowledge when the Holy Spirit is involved in our lives. It may be, however, that it is something He wants to use us for a lot or only from time to time. As with tongues or prophecy, the more we are prepared to learn and develop this gift the more God can trust us and use us.

THE BIBLE SAYS

1 Corinthians 12:4-11,31   Mark 16:20   John 4:13-19
1 Corinthians 13:1-2   1 John 2:20

ACTIVITY: How do we receive a word of knowledge?

LEADER'S NOTE:

In small groups ask the group to discuss how we can receive a 'word of knowledge'. This may include how God may communicate, how we know it is from Him, how we make ourselves receptive to hearing from Him regarding others.

Report back as a whole group.

It is important to mention (as with prophecy), the need to learn and operate in this way under the 'covering' and guidance of a leader/spiritual mentor.

KEYS FOR WORDS OF KNOWLEDGE

- Remember a word of knowledge is for a purpose.//dummy
- As with prophecy allow God to give you pictures, words, a sense about a situation or person.
- Regularly ask the Holy Spirit to use you to help others, show the power of God, and bring others to salvation through using words of knowledge.
- Begin with general truths about a person or situation and with practice, words of knowledge will become more detailed and specific.
- A word of knowledge often demands an action to follow, e.g. when it is about an injury or illness we should pray for the person if they are willing.

PRACTICAL

Encourage the group (or small groups, each with a leader if more appropriate) to take a minute to close their eyes and ask God for a word of knowledge for another person in the group. Invite volunteers to say what they have received.

It is important that the individuals are supported and guided in this. Usually someone will ask if anyone can relate to the word of knowledge, e.g. "I believe someone here has a problem with their big toe" or "Is someone here very worried about a family member?". There may be an immediate response and the person who brought the word of knowledge can be encouraged and supported to pray for that person with the whole group.

If no one responds, be encouraging and maybe come back to it/explain later what may be happening - ask God yourself.

ACTION PLAN

LEADER'S NOTE:
Encourage the group to write down at least one way to grow in the use of words of knowledge this week.

6. WORSHIP

"For God is Spirit so those who worship Him must worship in Spirit and in Truth."

John 4:24

INTRODUCTION

God is the reason we exist. He created us. He sent Jesus when we were lost and separated from Him through our rebellion. He is totally loving, faithful and consistent. When we consider who He is we cannot fail to see that He is the only one truly worthy of worship – the worship of every human being.

In worship we offer words, music, our bodies, all we have, our whole life, to the King of Kings. He becomes the focus of our attention as we take time to worship Him at specific times but also continually in our lives.

Worship is a decision. It is not an emotional response or a practised pattern or format, but involves our emotions and mind, being led by our spirit.

We glorify God and as we do so He draws us close to Himself to enjoy the wonderful relationship He intended at the beginning of time. We share intimate moments of time which will one day last for ever.

THE BIBLE SAYS

Revelation 4:8-11   Matthew 4:10   Exodus 20:4-5   Psalm 29:2

KEYS FOR WORSHIP

- Be yourself.
- Spend time alone worshipping God with words.
- Use CDs to take you into worship.
- Worship can involve silence.
- Listen to God while worshipping.
- Picture yourself before God.
- Consider your life as worship - how will this affect what you do?

ACTIVITY 1: What does worship involve?

LEADER'S NOTE:

As the whole group or in smaller groups, ask the question: "What does worship include?"

Possible answers may be: singing, loving God, dance, prayer, bowing down, honouring, sacrifice, praising, respecting, being humble before God, offering, music, whole life, obedience, etc.

ACTIVITY 2: Words of worship

LEADER'S NOTE:

Ask the group individually to write down words of worship to God.

Encourage them to consider God as creator and all powerful, but also as a loving God who wants an intimate relationship with us.

Encourage the use of words of worship in prayer or while singing in worship in their everyday lives.

PRACTICAL

Worship together.

Include a keyboard player or guitarist who is used to leading worship. Prepare one or two songs but include a time of free worship where the individuals can sing out to God in their native language or tongues.

It is good to have a few leaders involved in the session who could bring Scripture in and maybe sing out prophetically.

Although this must be a genuine time of worship, it is good to include different aspects of worship as examples of the diversity and place for different expressions.

It will also be helpful to bring explanation at times during the worship if this is done appropriately and doesn't break the flow.

ACTION PLAN

LEADER'S NOTE:

Encourage the group to desire to become more involved in worship in the church but also on their own. Ask them to consider and write down at least one action they will take.

7. Powerful TESTIMONY

"...and if someone asks about your Christian hope, ALWAYS be ready to explain it."

1 Peter 3:15

INTRODUCTION

God has done so much in our lives. If you have only been a Christian a very short time you might not have many examples to speak of, but the very fact of your salvation speaks of the most important thing He has done for you. Telling people why and how you became a Christian is one of the most powerful things you can pass on to others.

Our testimony as a witness to who God is and how He has impacted us can change others' lives. Other people cannot argue with what has happened to us as individuals. A testimony is speaking truthfully about our lives generally or specifically, or about a certain event. It is conveyed through words or actions to another or group of people.

Our testimony gives glory to God and focuses people on Him and not on us. We need to be ready at any time to give our testimony which needs to be fresh and engaging.

THE BIBLE SAYS

Mark 16:15-18   Matthew 28:18-20   Romans 1:16
2 Timothy 1:8-9 (AMP)   2 Timothy 2:14 (AMP)

KEYS FOR GIVING A TESTIMONY

- Be yourself.
- Regularly spend time considering what God has done in your life.
- Keep things simple when speaking about your life/experience.
- Use testimony that is appropriate to the person you are talking to.
- Don't use religious words/terminology that would be unfamiliar to a non-Christian.
- Look for connections with the other person and be relevant.
- Consciously think about glorifying God and the outcomes of your conversation/action.

ACTIVITY 1: What can I speak to others about?

LEADER'S NOTE:

Ask the group to individually consider and write down what testimony of God's work in their lives they could talk to others about. Remind them about purpose; it is not to focus on ourselves to show the other how good we are, or even to enjoy having someone listen to our achievements, it is about connecting the other person to God. Briefly ask for volunteers to say what they have written down - limit it to subjects not the stories.

ACTIVITY 2: Why should I speak to others

LEADER'S NOTE:

In groups or pairs, ask the group to discuss what the purpose of testimony is. Encourage them to consider the purpose of a witness in court as they do this.

Report back and discuss as a whole group. Possible responses may include:

- To share real like experiences
- To make the Gospel personal
- To help a person see how God can be involved in the life of a human being
- To show we can have a relationship with God
- To leave the other person with questions about their eternity, etc

PRACTICAL: What I learnt

In pairs ask the group to tell their partner how they became a Christian.

Encourage discussion about this. How did it feel to speak? How did it feel to listen? What have you learnt from the exercise? What impacted you about what was said?

Encourage the group members to find out what impacted the other person about what they said, whether that be tone, content, a particular fact etc. As they discover how or why their testimony was impacting remind them to develop/use this in the future.

Things to consider when giving a testimony: language, keep it short, do not condemn, it must be from the heart, make it relevant

ACTION PLAN

LEADER'S NOTE:

Encourage the group to make plans:

1. How to prepare for giving testimony
2. When they will speak to someone in the near future
3. Frequency - How often they will intentionally speak to someone

8. Spiritual PURPOSE

"There are different kinds of spiritual gifts, but the same Spirit is the source of them all."

1 Corinthians 12:4

ACTIVITY 1: What is meant by ministry? (not in student manual)

LEADER'S NOTE:

In small groups or pairs, ask the group to discuss and write down what is meant by 'ministry'. Invite the group to report back on their discussion.

Possible results include:

- What God calls us to do
- Serving the church
- Five-fold ministry
- Ministering in the spiritual gifts
- Serving the kingdom of God

N.B. It is a good idea to do this activity at the start of the session

INTRODUCTION

The Holy Spirit is involved in drawing us to the truth of our need for salvation. He then becomes part of our life at that point of new birth and fills us with power to fully experience and live the new life we gain. The Holy Spirit actively helps us as we use the Bible, pray, worship, make choices, face challenges, and in fact wants to be involved in every part of our lives. God always intended for us to be able to experience a constant and close relationship with Him.

The Holy Spirit also gifts us with special abilities in certain areas which will give us what we need to fulfil our unique purpose. It is important to know what we are specifically gifted to do as this will help us to determine our "calling" (area of ministry or church life). We will obviously be involved in many things as a Christian, but we will all be stronger in some areas than others. For example one person may be very musical and be able to sing which God wants to use in worship but the same person may not be gifted to a great degree in teaching the Bible.

When looking at gifts it is also important to bear in mind that we may have natural abilities which we may not connect with spiritual things but God has gifted us in those areas for a purpose other than what we may naturally think. For example the gifted person in music and singing can be an excellent performer but miss what God intended that gift to fulfil.

THE BIBLE SAYS

1 Corinthians 12:1,12-27 (See the Message Bible)   1 Timothy 4:14-15
2 Timothy 1:6-7   1 Peter 4:10-11

ACTIVITY 2: *What am I good at? What do I really enjoy?*

LEADER'S NOTE:

Ask the group to individually consider and write down what they are good at (backed up by others' opinions) and also what they really enjoy.

If there are things that fit into both categories it is likely that these areas are God-given gifts to be used to fulfil what God has called us to do.

KEYS FOR MINISTRY

- Pray asking God to show you the areas of your life He wants to use.
- Consider what you are good at (that others see) and what you enjoy (are passionate about). This is often where your gifting lies.
- Practically look to develp your gifts.
- Get involved in areas of service that involve using a gift and learn from others.
- Study around the area of your gifts.
- Pray about your gifts and submit them to the control of the Holy Spirit.
- Remember timing - God can have us in training for some time.

PRACTICAL: *Survey*

Carry out a Spiritual Gifts Survey which helps people discover their areas of ministry. Contact the author if you don't have suitable materials for this.

ACTION PLAN

LEADER'S NOTE:

Encourage the group to make plans to develop the ministry areas highlighted in the survey and write down what they will do.

E.g. speak to a leader about it, learn more about the area, pray about the area.

9. Positive INFLUENCE

"In the same way, let your good deeds shine out for all to see so that everyone will praise your heavenly Father."

Matthew 5:16

INTRODUCTION

The Bible tells us that God desires that all people should be saved and come back into relationship with Him. He also desires that the world we live in should become righteous and holy – meaning under His control and free from the power and control of the devil and evil. We are to partner with Him to bring about His purposes in the earth today.

Prayer is an important factor in bringing the world's systems and people's lives under the influence of the Kingdom of God, but we, in what we do and how we do it, can also influence this either positively or negatively.

Godly influence can be on different levels beginning with the people we come into contact with. It then can extend to how we influence our families, work place or schools and neighbours, and then even our communities, country and the world.

We are to be ambassadors of the Kingdom of God and play our part by influencing this world to turn it to righteousness.

THE BIBLE SAYS

Matthew 6:9-10   Proverbs 14:34(AMP)   Matthew 5:13-16   Philippians 2:14-15
Psalm 71:15,18b,19   2 Corinthians 5:20

KEYS FOR INFLUENCE

- Be yourself.
- Be relevant.
- Be good at your job.
- Consider how you come across to others.
- Pray for openings in your community where you can be a godly influence, e.g. a neighbourhood watch group or a school governor.
- Guard your words - be positive, encouraging, a team player, etc. Don't gossip.
- Ask the Holy Spirit to use you and speak through your actions as well as your words.
- Ask for words of wisdom so you can influence situations by bringing answers.

ACTIVITY 1: Who do I influence?

LEADER'S NOTE:
Ask the group to individually consider who they influence and then discuss the results as a group.

Expected answers may include:
Spouse, children, extended family, friends, colleagues, neighbours, friends, acquaintances, e.g. hairdresser, car mechanic, people we meet randomly.

The discussion will also bring up the point that we influence in different ways - some good, some bad. End with the idea that it is good to influence intentionally.

ACTIVITY 2: How best to influence

LEADER'S NOTE:
In small groups ask the group to discuss and write down ways of influencing others/groups/decision making, in the best ways.

Encourage them to be thinking about what the work of God's Kingdom is.
- Being positive
- Being a person of integrity
- Serving
- Giving
- Being wise
- Working well and hard
- Being well informed

Remember, being an influence involves being in places of influence. This discussion may move to talking about being in places of influence in the community/nation, e.g. education - school governor, head teacher, voluntary sector, community groups/partnerships, local government - councillor, Government - lobbying, MP

PRACTICAL:

Discuss with the group three areas in which we can be of influence: everyday life, work, local area/community.

Ask the group to consider which one of those they want to explore more then break up into three groups - one for each area.

In the groups, discuss how we can influence and what we can do practically over the next few months to move towards being a positive influence for God, His Kingdom and righteousness in the area being discussed.

ACTION PLAN

LEADER'S NOTE:
Encourage the group to write down at least one change they will individually make to become an intentional influencer.

10. RECAP / REVIEW / REFOCUS

ACTIVITY:

LEADER'S NOTE:
Give the group five minutes to consider individually what they have learnt, what has changed in their life due to this course and any questions they have.

What have I learnt?

_____

_____

What has changed in my life?

_____

_____

Questions

_____

_____

LEADER'S NOTE:
Spend the session discussing the questions and successes in people's lives over the last nine session.

Pray for each person as appropriate.

Discuss the future and what they will do next as we need to be continually learning in order to grow in our knowledge and relationship with God and spiritually.

ACTION PLAN

LEADER'S NOTE:
Encourage the group to consider and write down three goals relating to what they have learnt over the past weeks. These need to be S.M.A.R.T. goals. Help them to think through how to do this.

Specific **M**easurable **A**ttainable **R**ealistic **T**ime related

SUGGESTED READING

Brian Mulheran, (2002), **Jesus, Author & Finisher**, Synergy Publishers

Dutch Sheets, (1996), **Intercessory Prayer**, Ventura, CA: Regal Books

Stormie Omartian, (2001), **Praying God's Will For Your Life**, Thomas Nelson Publishing

Mahesh Chavda, (2001), **The Hidden Power Of Prayer And Fasting**, Destiny Image Publishers

Mahesh Chavda, (2001), **The Hidden Power Of The Believer's Touch**, Destiny Image Publishers

Selwyn Hughes, (2004), **Every Day With Jesus Bible**, Holman Bible Publishers

Kenneth and Gloria Copeland, (1999), **Pursuit Of His Presence**, Harrison House Inc.

Kenneth and Gloria Copeland, (1992), **From Faith To Faith**, Kenneth Copeland Ministries, Inc

Lester Sumrall, (1995), **The Making Of A Champion**, Whittaker House

Gary Chapman, (2004), **The Five Love Languages**, Northfield Publishing

Tommy Tenny, (1998), **The God Chasers,** Destiny Image Publishers

Tommy Tenny, (2003), **Finding Favour With The King**, Bethany House

Hannah Hurnard, (2005), **Hinds' Feet On High Places**, Kingsway Publications

Jackie Pullinger, (1980), **Chasing The Dragon**, Hodder and Stoughton Ltd

Tony Anthony, (2004), **Taming The Tiger**, Authentic Media

C.S. Lewis, (1997), **Mere Christianity**, Harper Collins

Benny Hinn, (1993), **Power In The Blood**, Word Publishing

Tim LaHaye, (1998), **How To Study The Bible For Yourself**, Harvest House Publishers

Bill Hybels, (2001), **Too Busy Not To Pray**, Inter-Varsity Press

David Spear (Ed.), (2002), **Jesus' Blueprint For Prayer**, Discovery House Publishing

Stevan Williamson, (1995), **Who's Afraid Of The Holy Ghost?**, Harrison House Inc.

Henri J. M. Nouwen, (2003), **The Return Of The Prodigal Son**, Darton, Longman and Todd Ltd

Andrew Murray, (1982), **God's Will: Our Dwelling Place**, Whittaker House

Floyd McClung, (1985), **The Father Heart Of God**, Kingsway Publications Ltd

Ulf Ekman, (1994), **The Church Of The Living God**, Word Of Life Publications

Rick Warren, (2002), **The Purpose Driven Life**, Zondervan

John Bevere, (2006), **Driven By Eternity**, FaithWords

Francis Chan, (2008), **Crazy Love**, David C Cooke

ABOUT THE AUTHOR

Ruth Lewis and her husband Simon have pastored and taught new Christians for a number of years within CityCoast Church. She has worked in collaboration with the KickStart team to produce this course to bring a foundation of truth for new Christians.

Ruth has a passion to see everyone discover who God designed them to be and go on to reach their full potential. She has experience in training, teaching and coaching using a variety of approaches, but always with the Bible at the centre and the Holy Spirit as the leader.

For more information regarding further resources and for training, please contact Ruth: ruth@kickstartresources.com

For further Kickstart resources visit www.kickstartresources.com
or email: info@kickstartresources.com

ABOUT CITYCOAST CHURCH

CityCoast is a church committed to leading people to Christ and equipping them to reach their God given potential in every area of their life. It is part of the Christian Outreach Centre movement of churches and was established in 1993 by Pastors Ashley and Ruth Schmierer. CityCoast church is led by Senior Pastors David and Jackie Harland.

CityCoast Church is called to:
* Worship God in spirit and in truth
* Love one another unconditionally
* Demonstrate the love of God for our community and lead people to Jesus
* Teach and train people in Biblical Christian living
* Act as a Christian influence in our community
* Put prayer at the heart of everything we do

www.citycoastchurch.co.uk

NOTES